Come Meet Some SEALS

By Beth Wise

S

Sadlier-Oxford

A Division of William H. Sadlier, Inc.

New York, New York 10005-1002

Come meet some seals.
But bring your coat.
It's freezing here!

Fur and blubber keep seals warm.
These little seals have fur
as white as snow!

But not all seals live where it's cold.
Come meet some seals on a sunny beach.

These seals get very hot.
But they find ways to beat
the heat.

5

Shh! These seals are sleeping.
Seals need to rest just like you.

Seals need to eat too!

A fish is a fine meal for a seal.

More Facts About
SEALS

Some seals can dive almost 2,000 feet.

Seals are born on land. Baby seals are called pups.

Some seals take long trips in the sea. Other seals seem to stay in the same place.